MAKING CHOICES

MARGARET SILF
ON
MAKING
CHOICES

A LION BOOK

A Lion Book
an imprint of
Lion Hudson plc
Mayfield House, 256 Banbury Road,
Oxford OX2 7DH, England
www.lionhudson.com
ISBN 0 7459 5133 3

First edition 2004
10 9 8 7 6 5 4 3 2 1 0

A catalogue record for this book is available
from the British Library

Typeset in 11/13 Goudy Old Style
Printed and bound in Malta

Contents

'It's our choices, Harry, that show us what we truly are, far more than our abilities.'
J.K. Rowling

Decisions, decisions!

Not just half a dozen, but scores, even hundreds of
   them, every day.

The range of choices we face in daily life
seems to grow exponentially,
and so does the accompanying stress.

Making choices has become something of a full-time activity
in an increasingly complex world.
It's a skill that is demanded of us constantly in our
   everyday living.

Is it something we can learn to do well?
Or is it just a matter of reacting more or less blindly to the
   demands of the moment?

And is there anything we can do to reduce some of the stress
   that life's unending choices place upon our time and our
   quality of life?

The aim of this little book is to help make the task of making choices less stressful, more focused and more fruitful.

It makes use of a few simple tools that combine the wisdom of ancient spiritual traditions with the commonsense of the twenty-first century.

It explores five aspects of choice-making:

Clearing the decks. Some choices are far more important than others. Some are not really ours to make. How do we sift the wheat from the chaff?

Starting where you are. We can only make sound choices from the place we actually find ourselves, not from where we wish we were, or think we ought to be. How do we learn to be true to ourselves?

Reading the signposts. Life provides us with teachers. Wisdom from outside ourselves, and wisdom from within. How do we read these signposts?

Choosing for the best. How do we turn our compromises and collusions into choices that reflect the very best in us?

Seeing it through. Making a decision is one thing. Implementing it is another. What if we make mistakes? Can we change course if we get things wrong?

Using the book

This is a book for browsing.
The kind of book that you might pick up
when you are facing a major decision,
or feeling overwhelmed by lots of minor ones.

Depending on where you are right now,
you will find different aspects of the art of choice-making
helpful. Use the contents page and the running headings
to find the section that most speaks to where you find
yourself.

It is a book of suggestions, not a rule book.
There is no 'answer book' for dealing with life's choices.
In every case we have to work it out for ourselves.
The solutions that work in life are the ones we discover for
ourselves, not the ones we find in the books.

So blend anything you find helpful in these pages
with a large measure of your own experience and your own
life-wisdom.

This book offers you a mixing bowl and a few spoons,
and the encouragement to trust the processes of your own
heart and mind.

Clearing the decks

Do you have to engage with every choice that presents itself?

If you look closely at the way you make your choices, you may notice certain patterns.

Some issues are important to you. You engage with them and make your choices about them.

Some issues go beyond your own control. You have to leave the choices, at least in part, to others. You delegate the choosing to people you trust to make choices on your behalf.

Some issues may be important, but also potentially uncomfortable or even painful. It can be tempting to sweep the matter under the carpet and hope it will go away. This avoids the immediate need to make a choice, but it can be storing up much more difficult choices for the future.

Some issues are simply not worth spending any time or energy on.

Before getting too deeply involved with a particular choice, it's worth looking at where it slots in on this kind of scale.

Sorting the wheat from the chaff

Our choices in life don't all carry equal weight. But, in practice, we tend to react to every choice-situation with the same basic 'fight or flight' mechanism. We either throw ourselves into the choosing, or we duck out of it, without too much thought about what we are doing.

A quick mental checklist may help you to sort out the wheat from the chaff:

Is this issue worth spending any time or energy on? If not, let it go and make space for the things that *do* matter.

Is this choice really down to you, or is it someone else's responsibility? Are you wasting your energy on things you can't change anyway, or on things beyond your range of influence? If so, let it go and make space for things that *are* your responsibility.

When the chaff is cleared,
you should be able to recognize more clearly
the choices you really do need to make,
including, perhaps, a few you might prefer to avoid.

The rest of this book suggests a few ways of approaching the choices that matter.

But first let's look at the art of letting go of the things that are simply cluttering up our minds unnecessarily.

Does this choice really matter?

How do you decide whether an issue matters to you or not?

This will probably be largely down to intuition, but a few key questions may be helpful:

Is this issue going to make any real difference to your own life or the life of anyone else? Will it affect anyone's safety or well-being?

If the answer to these questions is 'No', you still have a choice about whether to engage with the issue or not. The next question might be:

What will happen if you do nothing?

The consequences of doing nothing are either acceptable to you or not. If you don't like the result of doing nothing, then you *do* need to grapple with the issue. If you are indifferent to the consequences, you can still choose whether or not to involve yourself with the issue. This will depend on your answer to the question:

Do you have the time, energy and inclination right now to make a choice about this matter?

Let's look at a real example.

It's seven in the evening. You are just relaxing when the phone rings. It's a cold call from someone suggesting that you change your electricity supplier.

Do you want to get involved with this choice at all?

How do our questions help?

First: would your choice make any difference to anyone, affecting their well-being or your own?

Only you can know this. Is it important to you or your family to make some possible saving here, or not? If your answer is yes, then this is an issue you should engage with.

If your answer is no, think about what will happen if you do nothing. In this case, nothing will happen. Your electricity supply arrangements will stay as they are.

But maybe tonight you feel like looking into this matter. Do you have the time and energy to do the sums right now? If so, fine. If not, a polite 'Thank you, but no thank you' may be in order.

Is this choice really down to you?

Many of the choices that surround us in life go well beyond our own sphere of influence. They are really a matter of teamwork. We have some input to the decision-making, but we also have to delegate many of the choices involved to others.

In the nation, we choose our representatives; we choose whether to protest about certain issues; we don't choose the basic rate of income tax or the level of the education budget. If we don't like what we get, we can choose our representatives differently at the next election.

In the family, we choose our children's schools; we don't choose the way they are taught. If we don't like what we get, we can choose a different school.

So we make some basic choices ourselves, and we necessarily leave other choices to people who have the specialist skills and training to make them on our behalf.

The art is to discern what we can, and should, be making choices about, and what we can, and must, leave to others.

Are you trying to avoid something?

But what about those matters that you can and should be
   addressing,
but you would much rather not look at?
Issues that may demand courageous decisions,
active interventions,
diplomatic conversations,
or choices that may prove to be costly to you?

Take a cool look at the range of issues that are active for
you right now.

Perhaps a strained relationship with someone that you
really wish you could resolve but feel afraid of what might
happen if you do?

Perhaps a decision to give away something of your time or
energy or resources that will cause you a certain amount of
hardship?

Perhaps an impending change of job, or lifestyle, or
partnership that makes you feel apprehensive?

Be honest with yourself.

Is there anything you are trying to avoid?

Sometimes the fear of what lies ahead may be worse than any pain involved in actually making the decisive move.

For now, simply acknowledge that this matter is, indeed, an issue you need to address. The hints in the rest of this book may give you some help in making whatever hard choices need to be made.

Starting where you are

Beginning at Square One

Now you have cleared the field of those choices you really
   don't need to make at all,
there is room to look at the much more important questions:
the choices that *do* matter,
the choices where your response makes a difference.

Wherever you are going, in any issue,
you have to begin where you actually are, here and now.
This is your Square One.

'Square One' means the place where you are really *you*,
knowing how you really feel,
in the circumstances where you actually find yourself.

It doesn't mean:

where you wish you were, or
where you think you ought to be, or
where other people want you to be, or
where you might have been, if only...

It's all too easy to make important choices
under the influence of someone else's agenda.

It's even possible to spend a whole life
living out someone else's dream,
trying to conform yourself into the kind of person
someone else wants you to be.

You can only make sound choices when you begin from
a place where you feel you are being true to yourself and
true to how you *really* are.

Life is a bit like a game of snakes and ladders.

It can feel as though we land on each square by sheer chance, and then have to deal with whatever that square throws at us –

Maybe a ladder to take us a few steps forward.
Maybe a snake that drags us right back down again.

The 'dice' that determine where we land seem random and uncaring.
Overnight our fortunes can change.
We are caught up in a flux of uncertainty and unpredictability.

How can we make sensible choices amid such chaos?

Well, one thing we *can* do is start at Square One.
We can begin from where we are.
In fact, that is the only possible place to begin.

So what does Square One look like?

Square One is where circumstance has placed you.

You may be facing hard choices right now,
or on the brink of making life-changing decisions.

It's worth taking time to reflect on where you are really
  starting from.
It may not be quite as random as it feels.
It may be a place that holds gifts for you, as well as
  problems,
a place where you will find real resources
for making the haphazard journey through your life's choices.

Take time to explore your personal Square One.

What 'soil' are you growing in?

Where has life planted you?

What gifts does this soil contain, and what drawbacks?

Growing where you are planted

Sound decisions are grounded in this soil –
the soil of who you really are and where you find yourself
   in life.

Which doesn't mean that you can't change anything.
It simply means that this is the start point.

Your whole life is planted in a particular patch of soil:
your family, your upbringing, your education,
your likes and dislikes, your strengths and weaknesses.

This soil will influence your choices in life,
maybe more than you imagine.
It's a good idea to get to know it better,
to become more aware of what it contains.

The main thing it contains is your potential
   to become the unique person you truly are,
the fulfilment of God's dream for you,
and your own deepest dream for yourself.

All that potential is there in your Square One.
You won't find it anywhere else!

The ground of all your choices

Every choice in life also has its own Square One.

Before you begin to explore the choice itself, look at where
it has its roots.
The soil may seem like a set of constraints that limit your
decision.

For example:

The place where you live

The wider needs of your family and friends

Your abilities, that determine whether you could do a
particular job or not

Your likes and dislikes, that determine what you really *want*
to choose.

But in fact these constraints are also the soil that gives you
the resources you need to make your choice and carry it
out.

The soil keeps the plant contained in its circumstances.
The soil also contains the nutrients that allow the plant
to grow.

The river-banks limit the river's flow.
The river-banks also give the river the channel through
which it can flow to its destination.

Drawing on experience

One of the gifts we discover if we dig around at Square One is the memory of our own experience.

Experience is a great teacher.

It can warn us against going down certain paths that were not helpful in the past

It can encourage us to take risks, because in the past similar choices have led to good results

It can remind us that, although we have made plenty of mistakes in the past, we are still alive to tell the tale, and we may need to risk making mistakes in the future.

Try this little formula to test out new choices and decisions:

Have you ever been in this kind of situation before?

If so, how did you choose to respond at the time?

In the light of this experience, how do you choose to respond now?

Sometimes we need to break free from the habits and responses of the past.
Sometimes we can learn from them and build on them.
Only experience can show us the difference.

Look at any particular decision you are dealing with right now.

Where is your starting point – your Square One – on this issue?

What are the constraints?

Where do you find yourself in this issue?
Are you starting from where you truly are,
or are you trying to force yourself into a place where you think you ought to be?
Are you trying to fit yourself into a pattern that other people think you ought to fit?
Are you trying to work things out from a place where you wish you were,
or where you might have been if you had started from somewhere else?

What does your experience tell you?

Sit down with yourself, and ask yourself: where is the real you in all of this?

Beware of the 'if-onlys'

Take a long look at any if-onlys that may be lurking around.

If only I had followed so-and-so's advice last year…

If only I had finished my college course…

If only I had been born in another time, another place,
   another family…

The if-onlys are the worst enemies of the present moment,
and the present moment is your best friend in all your
   choice-making.

If-onlys will rob you of your last ounce of energy and take
   you absolutely nowhere.
They will send you off down every imaginable cul-de-sac.
They will leave you feeling frustrated and resentful.

The present moment is the source – and the only source –
of all the energy you need to make the best next move.

Start where you are.
And if you have already wandered off down some of those
   cul-de-sacs,
go back…
to Square One!

Beware of 'what-ifs'

Now take a look at another enemy of the present moment,
the *what-ifs*...

What if I get it all wrong, and make things worse?
What if I speak my truth honestly, and make enemies?
What if I challenge this situation and put my job at risk?
What if people laugh at me?

The *what-ifs* have two faces.

They can be friends,
helping us to recognize our options,
warning us about possible outcomes.

But if we let them bully us,
if we start to fill up with fear in their presence,
they are not friends, but enemies.

Caution is a friend of our decision-making.
Undue fear is its enemy.

The difference between reasonable caution and excessive fear
is something we can't work out in our head, but we feel
   in our gut.

So listen to your gut feelings.
Is there turmoil down there? Is fear taking over?

Just notice your reaction,
if the *what-ifs* are getting too powerful.
You can actively choose to give them less power,
as you move on in your task of making a choice.

You are what you choose

Remember those join-the-dots puzzles you used to do when
you were a child?

At first sight they just looked like a random scattering of
dots.
It was impossible to guess what hidden picture the
dots contained.
The picture only began to emerge as you painstakingly
joined up the dots,
one at a time,
step by step.

Life is something of a join-the-dots mystery too.
Usually it's impossible to see any meaning in the chaos of
our circumstances,
or any pattern emerging out of the mess of everyday living.

Yet underneath it all, inside it all, a pattern *is* emerging.
A meaning *is* evolving.

We only see it with hindsight.

Sadly, the pattern is sometimes not recognized until the
funeral service,
when we think back over a person's life,
and notice what kind of unique difference it made.

While we live, we are still picking our way forward, dot by dot.
The way we make our choices is the way we make
those joins.
Every choice along the way makes a difference to the
picture that will eventually emerge.

We really want the true picture to emerge at the end
    of the day.
This is what we would like to leave behind on Planet Earth:
A true footprint of our true self.

Maybe even a footprint that will help others to find their
    own true path in life.

But all we can really influence is where the next line goes.
We can only choose the next dot,
    and hope that it is helping to shape the true picture,
    and not obscuring it or distorting it.

Is it just a matter of 'fingers-crossed' and hope we get it right?
Or is there a sounder guide than blind hope, as we take
    each next step?

Preparing the ground

Children's join-the-dots puzzles are easy to follow.
It's fairly obvious where the next line should go.

It's not like that in the real world.
The next line could go almost anywhere,

so how do we choose?

We don't know – and can't yet imagine – the full picture.
But we do know Square One.
We know at least a bit about who we truly are,
and what we truly value.

This gives us a head start in choosing the next step.

There are some useful tools to help us make each new
    choice along the way –
the big decisions and the apparently trivial ones.
Together they are forming and shaping 'who you are'.

But we begin with a little preparation...

Decisions, like other projects, tend to do better when we
   prepare for them.
The bigger the decision, the more preparation is needed.

The way you prepare depends a lot on the kind of choice
   that is on the agenda.

Some are long term, that demand a lot of thought.
Some are 'instants', that you can't prepare for at all.
Some offer a whole variety of options.
Some offer only two: 'Take it or leave it.'

Take a look at any choices you are dealing with right now:
you might find it helpful to make a note of them.
Just to name them to yourself is a good way of beginning to
   prepare the ground.

Reviewing the options

Important decisions require some care.
There are things we can do to prepare ourselves better to
  make a good choice.

We can set out the options…

It's worth putting them down on paper if you can.
What choices do you actually have in this situation?

Go through them one by one.

Are any of them unrealistic?

Are they impossible for practical reasons?

Are they incompatible with your existing responsibilities and commitments?

Do they go against the voice of your conscience?

Exclude the unrealistic options from your list.

Now you have a clearer view of what the different possibilities really are in this matter.

This is the start point for making your choice.

Making snap decisions

Snap decisions don't give you the luxury of time and space
to think.
Many of them will seem relatively trivial
but they may have a profound effect on other people.

How you choose to react to a remark or a situation may
make the kind of difference to someone else that they
never forget,
either in thankfulness or resentment.

We can't prepare for snap decisions.
But when we nurture the habit of being careful about the
bigger things,
the smaller things will begin to follow the same kind of
pattern, though we will be unconscious of this.

The care you expend on your bigger choices will colour
your 'instants' too.
When you are true to the best in yourself in the big things,
that same integrity will weave through the small things.

But:

Beware of any pressure to make snap decisions
in situations that you know really need more time and
thought.

Better, by far, to resist such pressure
than to live with unwanted consequences that could have
been avoided.

Reading the signposts

Tuition, and intuition

Let's assume…

you know what kind of choice or decision you are facing;
you have cleared the field of non-essential factors, and
you feel you are starting from a place where you are being
true to yourself.

How can you move on?

Is there anywhere you can look for guidance?

There are two deep wells of wisdom
available to us all.
We can draw from them deeply and often.

Let's call them

'Tuition', and

'Intuition'.

Tuition is something we are given from outside ourselves.
It comes from our parents and family,
our culture and tradition,
our teachers and employers,
our friends and our critics.

All these people play a part in instructing us as to what to do,
how to choose, in particular situations.

Intuition is something that dwells within us.
It is an inner wisdom that prompts us gently about the
right course to pursue,
the better reaction to a situation.
It grows out of the values we hold dear,
the hidden springs of experience,
our hopes, dreams and desires.

It isn't always rational.
It isn't meant to be.
It's the partner of our reasoning mind, not an opponent.

Tuition and intuition can work together to draw us
towards the better outcome, the wiser choice.

Who are your teachers?

Take time to notice the sources of tuition that help you in your decision-making.

Who are your role models, and why?
What values and guidelines did you learn from various teachers or wisdom figures in your life?

These values are probably guiding you more profoundly than you imagine.
Take time to become more aware of them.

Some of the best tuition comes from our critics.
Those who disagree with us will tell us the truth, without flattery.
And truth is a great tutor.

Just as children learn more from their mistakes at school than from their perfect scripts,
so we can learn more from our truthful critics than from those who only tell us what they know we want to hear.

How do you feel about criticism?
Some of it (but not all!) may be more helpful than you dare to think.

But not everything we are taught is either good or helpful.

Many people grow up with an image of themselves as an under-achiever, for example, or a misbehaving child.

Unconsciously they take this bit of 'teaching' into their adult decision-making. They stay in the role that was once assigned to them.

They are not starting from where they really are, but from where someone else (parents, teachers, employers) once thought they were.

Take a cool look at how *you* see yourself,
and where *your* learned reactions are coming from.

Which do you value, and want to keep?

Which would you like to set aside now, and move beyond?

The choice is yours!

Learning from others

A different kind of guidance comes from those who have faced similar decisions before us.

No two people's experience is ever the same but, even so, we can share some of the learning curves with each other.

A person who has had to deal with some difficulty – maybe a specific health problem, or hardship, redundancy, marital breakdown, or financial loss – will often develop real empathy for others in the same situation.

Self-help groups show how this works in practice.
The wisdom of the group is greater than the sum of the wisdom of its individual members.

If we need to choose a new washing machine, we may ask friends and neighbours for their recommendations.

Why are we so hesitant to do the same when we are dealing with more serious matters?

Can I trust my advisers?

To seek guidance and advice from each other is simply a
part of what it means to be human,
and part of an interrelated, interdependent web of life.

But…
How do we know which recommendations we can trust?
We are swamped with 'guidance', telling us what we should
    eat, drink, wear and think.
We know instinctively that much of this kind of guidance
    is unreliable.

Why?

Because it has a hidden (or not-so-hidden) agenda.
It is given with the intention of making us part with our
    money,
or of gaining some kind of control over us.

Unfortunately, hidden agendas may lurk in apparently
    innocent advice too.
They are so tricky precisely because they *are* hidden.
Before you act on guidance from outside, ask yourself:

Does the person offering me this advice have anything to
    gain if I accept it,
or anything to lose if I reject it?

A 'yes' to either should trigger a warning bell.

The only kind of guidance or advice that is truly objective
    is that which is offered in genuine freedom of heart.

Can I trust my intuitions?

We have sources of guidance and wisdom deep within
  ourselves too,
though sometimes we are reluctant to trust them.

You could think of your own intuition as a kind of inner
  compass.
If you reflect on it, you will recall times when you have
  followed it, and it has served you well.

Most of us know intuitively when we are being true to
  ourselves,
and when we are walking paths that don't feel right.

We know when the inner compass is reading true,
when we are doing what feels right for us,
responding to life from our true centre.

Take a moment to remember any times when you felt this
  was happening.
What was the issue in question at the time?
How did you choose to react?
How did you feel at the time?
What was the outcome?

It's important to notice and remember these times when
  we are 'living true'.
They are like an imprint on our hearts,
a blueprint of how it feels when the inner compass is
  registering true north.

But there are, inevitably, many, many times when the
   opposite is true.

We make choices from somewhere that is not the true
   centre of ourselves.

Perhaps we do something to please someone else,
even though we feel a bit uneasy about it.

Perhaps we act out of fear.
The *what-ifs* bully us into doing less than our best.
The *if-onlys* freeze us into regret, and steal the energy we
   need to move on.

Perhaps we let ourselves 'go with the flow',
even though in our hearts we know that 'the flow' is going
   the wrong way.

Or perhaps we settle for less, for mediocrity, for the safer
   option,
even though deep down we want to take the risk of going
   for what we really desire.

Reading the inner compass

Often the inner compass wobbles!

We notice this because we start to feel anxious,
to sense an inner unrest,
to catch ourselves trying to justify what we are doing,
or looking for someone to blame.

We are human, and we all know how this feels.
Take a moment to recall how such times have been for you.
Don't judge yourself.
Judgment is never helpful.
It focuses your energy in the wrong place –
on yourself, rather than on the matter in hand.

Instead, just notice the pattern of how it feels when your
    inner compass is wobbling.
Recognizing the symptoms is a major step towards
    overcoming them.

Then, when the compass wobbles in future,
you will be more aware of what is going on in your heart,
more free to choose to act against whatever is causing
    the wobbles.

The remembered experience of how it feels
when the compass is registering true north
becomes part of your store of inner wisdom.

The more we follow our intuitions when they are
    registering true, the easier it gets.

Inner wisdom is a resource that grows with experience.

Trusting the inner compass

When you are on a mountainside and the fog comes down,
the only way to be sure of finding the right track
is to use your map and compass.

But, as many climbers have learned to their cost,
we tend to think we know better than the compass.

The compass points one way, but surely, we think, we came
up the path over *there*.
Perhaps there is something wrong with the compass.

And so we rationalize our own faulty memories of where
the path might be.
Or perhaps we talk each other into taking a wrong turning.
And perhaps we end up in the wrong valley...
or worse!

When we are making important decisions,
we need to *trust* the inner compass.

It will guide us more surely than our reactions to the
immediate conditions,
or the advice of panicking friends.

Listening to our feelings

What helps us to read this mysterious inner compass?

It may surprise you to learn that your feelings can be your
  teachers.

Feelings? Such fickle things?
Indeed, they *are* fickle,
but they tell us the truth, nevertheless,
about where we really are at the time.

Imagine a sandy beach.
You want to walk there safely,
but part of the beach is composed of quicksands.
In other parts there is rock beneath the sand.
The sand looks the same everywhere,
so how do you know where the rock is,
and where the quicksands are?

The answer is usually –
'From experience!'

You learn where the quicksands are
by *feeling* your feet being sucked down,
and the fear that grips you when this happens.

You notice where it is safe to walk
by *feeling* the firm rock supporting your steps.

You won't forget those feelings.
They will be your trustworthy guides,
whenever you walk on the beach.

Life is a bit like that beach.

It is full of hidden hazards,
quicksands that suck us down into the depths of despair.

But it also has areas of solid rock,
where we know we are on firm ground
and we can walk with confidence.

The key to discovering the nature of the terrain begins
with our *feelings*.

It can be very helpful to cultivate the habit of reflecting
back over the events of the passing days.

It helps us to begin to live *reflectively*.

Living reflectively

Take time to *reflect back* over how the day has been…

What happened to make you feel you were on shaky
  ground?
Notice any feelings of being inwardly unsteady.
Now notice what gave rise to them.

Perhaps something was said that caused a bad atmosphere
  to develop.
Perhaps you reacted out of fear, or a false desire to please
  someone,
and afterwards you felt discontented with yourself,
or uneasy about the outcome of your choice.

These movements are like the quicksands.
They are strong warnings that we are not walking on solid
  ground.
Notice them –
notice where they come from.
Maybe a particular relationship regularly drains you of energy,
or undermines your confidence.
Maybe some issue in your life is filling you with apprehension.

Just notice these connections.
Your feelings can point to the quicksands in your life,
and help you to avoid the shaky ground in future.

What happened to make you feel you were walking on a
   solid foundation?

Perhaps you made a choice and felt intuitively that the
   right thing had been done or said
in the right way,
at the right time.

Perhaps events proved again that a particular friend is reliable,
or that some activity or task in your life draws out the best
   in you and renews your energy,
or that some relationship always leaves you feeling more
   alive.

If you make a habit of reflecting back over the day,
you will learn to read the map of your circumstances,
and recognize what regularly tends to suck you down,
and what helps to move you on.

Feelings and reflection go together.
Feelings alone will not help you
unless you reflect on what they are telling you.

To listen to your feelings,
and then to reflect on their signals,
is to learn the art of *reflective living*.

Reflection like this only needs to take a few minutes,
but it can make a big difference
to your ability
to make wise choices.

Noticing any over-reactions

Over-reactions are another very sound guide to what is
   really going on in your heart.

Did you go over the top about anything during the day?
What triggered the reaction?
How do you feel about it with hindsight?

An over-reaction like this
is like the bubbles from a submerged shark.
It is a tell-tale sign that something bigger is lurking under
   the surface of what you see.

If you notice bubbles like this coming up in your day,
it may be very important to stop at that point,
and ask yourself – without judgment! –
Where are these bubbles really coming from?

If you lost your temper with a colleague,
or grumbled at the neighbour's children,
or came close to road rage with another driver,
where was this negative energy coming from?

Very often you will find that it isn't all it seems to be.
The driver who enrages you may actually be activating
    deeper reasons for your anger.

The girl who delays you in the supermarket,
by chatting needlessly to the person in front of you,
may actually be doing you a favour.
She may be the signal that warns you
that the pressures in your life are running dangerously high.

The gift of life's irritations

Life is full of minor and major irritations.
The irritant can be a pain –
but the pain itself can be the symptom of something more
  seriously wrong.

Pain is a blessing.
It is the body's early warning system
that something is wrong,
and needs attention, before it becomes a threat to health
  and life.

The irritants that get under our skin
and make us over-react,
can be blessings too.
They can be our inner early warning system
that something needs attention,
before it threatens our inner well-being,
our relationships,
or even our integrity.

The grit in the oyster
is the irritant that becomes the pearl.

Don't disregard the irritants of your daily life.
They may be shaping precious pearls of wisdom.

The gift of desire

An especially potent feeling is the feeling of *desire*.

The word 'desire' is charged with meaning.
What does it mean to *you*?

Desire has a bad press.
We tend to think that if we desire something,
it is probably something we ought not to want or to have.

But think about it:

Without desire we would never get up in the morning.
We would never have ventured beyond our own front door.
We would never have read a book or learned anything new.

No desire means no life, no growth, no change.
Desire is what makes two people create a third person.
Desire is what makes the crocus bulbs push up through the
   winter soil.

Desire is energy,
the energy of all creativity, the energy of life itself.

So let's not be too hard on desire.

What do you really want?

Can our desires help us to make wise choices?

It depends on how deep they go.

There are deep desires,
and there are shallow desires.

Shallow desires translate into wish lists.
They turn up for Christmas and birthdays.
We would like to have this, that and the next thing.
We could probably live happily without these things,
but if we are asked what we want,
then we can usually supply a list.

If your children or friends were to ask you,
'What would you like for your birthday?'
what would you say?
Just notice these wants and wishes.
Notice how deeply you feel about them.
What sacrifices would you be willing to make in order to
   gain what you want?

Now take a look at a deeper level of desiring.

Is there something you have always wanted to do, but
    never managed?
What are the unfinished dreams of your youth?
If you had your life over again, what would you change?
If you had only a few months to live, how would you spend
    the time?
If a significant sum of money suddenly came your way, how
    would you spend it?
If a fairy godmother granted you three wishes, what would
    they be?
Is there anything, or anyone, you would literally give your
    life for?

Take time to ponder one or more of these questions.
The responses you make to yourself,
provided they are your honest answers,
and not just the answers you feel you *ought* to give,
will be pointers to where your deepest desires are rooted.

Look closely, taking time to reflect on what you find.
There may be patterns in your desiring that help you
    understand more fully who you are,
and what makes you tick.

Sometimes our apparently superficial desires can lead us down to the deeper levels.

For example:

A friend tells you that he wants a country cottage.
'Why is that?' you might ask.

Given the opportunity, he might begin to unpack his reasons.

To get right away from my work at weekends…
To have an oasis of peace in my life…
To have a garden…
To have a place where I could spend quality time with my family…

And so on.

So this desire isn't just a self-centred 'I want!'

It has to do with deeper issues, such as:

A desire for peace, and a return to a more tranquil lifestyle.
A desire to deepen and nourish important relationships.
A desire to counteract the effects of stress.

These are deeper layers of desiring.

How do they affect the way we make our choices?

Well, these deeper layers are always there,
unconsciously affecting the way we shape our lives.

Any choices we make that go *against* our deepest desires
will leave us feeling uneasy and discontented.

The choices we make that *nourish* these deep desires
will leave us feeling more in harmony with ourselves and
those we love.

The deep desires
affect the smaller choices,
in ways we may not always recognize.

It matters, to recognize the shape of our deepest desires.
It helps us to make our everyday choices
in ways that align with our deeper desires and values.

And, ultimately, we will find inner peace most readily
if our own deeper desires and values
are in harmony, and not at odds, with
the deep desires, hopes and aspirations
of the whole human family,
and of all creation.

What is best for all of us is, ultimately, best for each of us.

Choosing for the best

Life's snakes and ladders

We've looked at the sources of wisdom and experience that
   help us make our decisions.

These provide signposts that we need in all our
   decision-making.
They are wells that nourish our ability to choose wisely,
and from which we can draw freely.

As we grow in self-awareness,
welcoming respectfully all that life has to teach us,
through history and through each other,
and learning to trust our own inner compass,
we become more and more equipped
to face the choices with which life confronts us,
and to negotiate the challenge of life's game of snakes and
   ladders.

We may not have any choice about the random events that
  land us in good or not-so-good places, day by day.

Some choices we face seem to drop us at the bottom
  of a ladder.
Things are looking good.
Chance has thrown us a golden opportunity.
All we need to do is climb.

In other situations the opposite is true.
The head of a snake is hissing in our direction.
If we're not careful, we may slide right down
where we never wanted to go.

Very often a particular choice has both these possibilities
  on one square –
the foot of a ladder and the head of a snake.

We have no choice about where circumstances cast us.
Do we have a choice about whether we climb the ladder,
or slide down the snake?

Let's investigate.

Climbing the ladders

The ladder is a shorthand way of describing all those issues
that invite us to live true to who we really are.
Ladders invite us 'up',
to go beyond our personal best,
to make the wise choice that makes a difference,
not just for ourselves, but for others.

The ladder asks us,
'What does the *best* in you choose to do?'

It may not be the easiest option.
It takes a real effort to put your foot on the first rung
of the ladder
and start to climb
towards that beckoning Best.

Often it would be much easier just to sit there on the
square of this day's routine,
and let the opportunity pass you by.

But if you can do it,
you won't regret it.
The best in you will grow stronger.
It will be easier to choose the better course next time.

You will do this best if you know where you are most likely
    to encounter the ladders in your life.

Take some time to reflect on any situations,
or relationships,
or activities, times or places,
that consistently draw out the best in you.
Name them to yourself.
Acknowledge their benevolent influence on you,
and reaffirm to yourself
the desire to be in partnership with them.

What might you do, specifically,
to nourish and strengthen the ladders in your life?
To focus your energy on the things that bring you closer
to the best in you?
To overcome any reluctance you may detect in yourself
to make the effort
of putting your foot on the first step
towards choosing the better route?

Next time you are facing a decision,
ask yourself,
'Is this the foot of a ladder?'

Handling the snakes

The snake is a symbol of all the slippery slopes
that lead us away from the best in us.

The seductive primrose paths
that distract us
and steal the energy we really need
to keep growing into the person we truly are.

The problem with the snakes is that
once you set one foot on top of the slide,
you are off down the slope
faster than you can think.

It takes no effort at all
to slide down the snake –
on the snakes and ladders' board,
just as in the adventure of life.

To avoid the slide down,
we have to deliberately act *against* the downward drag.

We do this best
when we are familiar with how the snakes look,
where they tend to lurk
and where we are personally most vulnerable to them.

So take the time,
and keep on taking the time,
to reflect on what the snakes mean for *you*.

Are there any situations,
or relationships,
or activities, times or places

where you know, from experience,
that you are likely to be pulled away
from your personal truth,
and make choices that are not worthy of the best in you?

Is there something you can do
to work actively against the effects of these influences
that are pulling you out of your true orbit?

Look at any choices you are facing.
Is there evidence of any snakes around the decision?
What might you do to counteract their effect?

Choosing the better

Ladders are not always simply good news.
Sometimes we have to choose
'the lesser of the evils'.
To choose well is to choose the best we can.

Snakes are not always simply bad news.
Often, in real life,
the snakes are just the 'less good'.
Often the choice lies between the good and the better.

The good can sometimes be the enemy of the better.

To choose well is to choose the better.

Maybe you are standing, even now,
on a square of your circumstances
that offers you both the bottom of a ladder
and the head of a snake.

Look closely at this particular situation,
this specific choice before you.
Name the snake in it,
and name the ladder.

What shape do they take?
What kind of distraction or temptation is this snake for you?
What kind of opportunity or challenge is this ladder for you?

Which will you choose?
Which does the *best* in you choose?

Listening to past experience

Take a trip through your memory bank.
Where, in your previous experience,
has this particular kind of snake,
this form of distraction or temptation, led you?

Is that where you want to go now?

Where, in your previous experience,
has this kind of a ladder,
this kind of challenge or opportunity, led you?

Is this where you want to go now?

If you knew you only had a short time to live,
which would you choose?

Remember, from your own experience,
the ladders give you energy.
They have the potential to make you more alive,
more truly who you are,
but you have to take the first step,
put your foot on the first rung.

The snakes will take you for all you've got!
They have the potential to deaden you
and impede your growth into who you truly are.
They can pull you down faster than you know,
but you have the choice
about whether to make the slide.

Some venomous snakes

Be alert especially for these common, and venomous,
  snakes…

False programming, that tells you
  you are no good… you'll never manage it…
  you'll never keep it up… you just haven't got it in you.

You may have been programmed like this as a child,
but you are not a computer.
You don't have to keep running the program.
You have a choice.

False securities, that tell you
  it's too risky… they might laugh…
  earn enough, own enough and you'll be fine,
  if you build enough defences, you'll be invulnerable.

External defences won't protect you.
Only your inner resources will give you solid ground.

False expectations, that…
  this new job, this new relationship, this new house
  will solve everything.

At the end of the day,
both the problem
and the solution
lie in your own hands,
and your own choices.

Testing your choices

There are some practical tools to help you check out your choices before doing anything irrevocable.

Let's look at a few of them:

The ripple effect test

The pros and cons test

The dry run test

The barometer test.

The ripple effect test

No one is an island.
What one person decides affects many others.

What you decide may cast ripples right across the
  world's pond.
It may decisively affect people you don't even know,
people not yet born,
and the planet those people will inhabit.

Take a look at the choice you are making.

As far as you are able to predict,
what effect might it have on you?

On those close to you?
Children,
partners,
parents,
friends,
colleagues,
neighbours?

What effect might it have on the wider population?
On your neighbourhood,
your workplace,
your community,
the rest of the world?

What effect might it have on creation as a whole?
On the planet, and all its creatures, and on generations
  still unborn?

The pros and cons test

For this exercise you will need paper and a pencil.
If your choice affects other people directly, you might want
    to do the exercise together.

Look at the various, realistic, options you have identified
    for this decision.

For each option, use a sheet of paper, divided down
    the middle.

On one side, list all the advantages of choosing in favour
    of this option.
On the other side, list all the disadvantages.

Repeat the process for each of your options.

At the end of the exercise, you will have a clearer picture
    of which option is the more favourable.

If more than one person is involved, this will also reveal
    the genuine desires and needs of the individuals concerned.

The dry run test

Give yourself enough time and space to 'live with' the
alternative scenarios of your decision in your
imagination.
'Enough time' means at least a couple of
days, more if necessary.

Say to yourself: I have firmly decided to do A.
Let the days take their course, as if Course A were fixed
and settled.
How do you feel about the consequences of choosing
Course A?
Is your inner compass registering true, or is it wobbling?
Notice especially any feelings of unease or tension.
These might be signs that Course A is not for you.
Notice any feelings of inner peace, even joy.
These might be suggesting that Course A is just right.

Now change over.
Do the same for Course B,
and for any further possibilities you have in mind.
Note down how you are feeling, in each case,
especially any thoughts or feelings
that seem to be warning you of possible
unwanted consequences.

So far, this is still just in your mind.
You haven't committed yourself to either of the options.
Let your own feelings and reactions be your guide.

The barometer test

Look at the choice you are trying to make, and the direction your decision appears to be going.

Suppose you could measure the quality of your choice on a barometer.

At the top of the scale is what the best in you would choose.

At the bottom of the scale is what the worst in you would choose.

On a scale of one to ten, where do you think your preferred choice would register on this barometer?
Be completely honest with yourself.

How do you feel about your assessment?
Are there any adjustments you would want to make to your decision now?

Remember that it isn't always realistically possible to choose the very best we would want to choose.
Don't be hard on yourself, but be honest!

Other techniques

A few other techniques can also help you to test your
   choices in advance:
Ask yourself how you would choose if you had only a short
   time to live.
It is said that the closer we approach the ultimate threshold,
the more clearly we focus on what really matters to us.
What really matters to you in this choice?

Ask yourself how you would advise someone you love,
if they were facing the choice that lies before you.
What might you want to say to this person,
and why?

Think of the person in your life whose opinion and values
   you most genuinely admire.
How do you think this person would advise you?

Remember, quite consciously, any times in the past when
   you have faced a similar kind of choice.
How did you choose then?
How do you feel about that choice in the past?
How does the experience affect the way you want to make
   your choice now?

Have you drawn a complete blank?

A wise friend once said to me,

'When you are trying to decide between A and B,
sometimes X is the answer.'

Do you feel totally stuck?
Do you really not know at all which option to go for?
Does every possible path leave you feeling confused and
   unsure of yourself?

This may be an indication that none of the possibilities
   you have identified
is the right course to follow.

Try letting them all go, and living for a day or two with the
   blank space they leave behind.

Just let things be.
Don't even think about the problem,
but keep your mind alert and open.
It may be that a very different course of action suggests
   itself to you.
Maybe something you had never even considered.

If so, try putting this new option through the
   discernment tests
and see what happens.

Can you get it wrong?

Of course we can get things wrong.
We are human.
To err is human.
The more we err, the more human we are!

If success means the perfect immediate solution for all
   concerned,
then most of the time we will fail.

But if success means becoming daily more true
to who we really are,
then actually we cannot fail.

Every time we choose what the best in us desires,
we grow a little bit closer to that 'best'.

Every time we make an unwise choice,
we enter into what is potentially
a new learning curve.

Learning from the mistakes

Like children,
we learn more from our mistakes
than from our perfect solutions.

Like creation,
we evolve through difficulty and challenge,
not through the easy times when there is nothing to
   stretch us.

Why do we so rarely learn from our mistakes?
Perhaps it's because we never admit that they are *our*
   mistakes.
We prefer to blame someone else,
another person, or our upbringing, or simply 'them'.

To own our mistakes
is to embrace our own potential
to grow better, wiser and more fully human.

Becoming what we choose

There is a creative dynamic at work in us,
constantly striving to weave something new and better
out of whatever we present,
growing our poor into better, and our good into best.
We can choose to work with it or against it,
but we can't opt out of it.
It is the dynamic of life
in an evolving universe.

But the opposite dynamic is also in evidence.
It is constantly striving
to pull our best down to mediocre
and our poor to worst.
We see its footprints in history,
and we know where it can lead.
We can choose to let it pull us out of our true orbit,
or we can choose to act against it.

It's our choices that make us who we are.
And in an evolving universe,
our choices make a difference
for all creation.

The world is bigger than our 'board',
and our personal game of snakes and ladders
is part of something much, much larger.
Just a part,
but a unique and essential part.

And sometimes the longest snakes we slide down
deliver us to the foot of the longest ladders,
a fresh starting place,
opening up a new angle on a problem
we thought we couldn't solve.

Seeing it through

Implementing your choices

To give a good talk,
you need about twenty times as long to prepare as to
deliver it.

The same is true when making choices.
The time taken to prepare may far exceed the time it takes
to implement your decision.

Even so, the hardest part of giving a talk
is actually standing there and giving it.

The hardest part of making a choice
is actually putting it into practice.

Now you have weighed all the options,
you have done all you can to check out the likely outcome
of your choice,
you have taken account of all the wisdom available to you,
you have listened to your own gut feelings, your intuitions,
your inner compass.

You have reached a conclusion.

What has to happen to make it a reality?

It may be that hard moves are needed,
or hard words
or hard feelings.

Maybe a draining, or even abusive, relationship has to
be ended.
People will get hurt.

Maybe a dependent person has to be liberated from such
dependency,
and maybe that person won't welcome the liberation at all.

Maybe the voice of truth has to be heard, where there
is deceit,
and maybe that will cost
what appears to be a good job,
a good reputation,
a comfortable life.

Or maybe past harm needs to be undone,
and apologies or reparations are called for,
and humility,
and the ability to start over again.

Hard choices

These are not easy places to be,
but they are human places,
and they are places of great growth.

Two very human qualities may be needed
in careful balance with each other.

The first is *honesty*,
integrity,
being true to who you really are.

The second is *empathy*,
compassion,
being sensitive to who the other person really is.

How will you implement your choice,
holding these two qualities in balance?

Look at your choice now in this light.
What has to happen to make it real?
Are you ready to meet the cost?

To be human – really human –
is costly,
but it is always worth the price.

Can you change your mind?

Life moves on.
Nothing is fixed.
Sometimes it is necessary to change your mind.
And sometimes it might be the worst possible thing to do.

How can you tell?

To change your mind about a wrong decision
is a sign of honesty.
It reveals the healthy humility of someone who has the
   grace to know
that they are not always right,
and the courage to admit it to others.

If you are experiencing regrets
about a choice you have made in your life,
how do you know whether you should reverse it,
assuming that reversal is still possible?

Changing course

First look at the nature of your regrets.

Are they about the actual choice you made?
Do you feel, now, that you genuinely chose the wrong
    course of action?
What are your reasons for feeling like this?

Have the consequences been harmful for yourself or
    for others?
Has the choice you made not led to the result you were
    hoping for?

Now ask yourself whether you *can* still change your choice.

If you changed the course of action you actually implemented,
how would this affect other people?
Would it undermine your existing commitments?
Would it impose extra burdens on others?
Who would benefit from the change of course?
As far as you can judge, would anyone suffer from it?

If you do change course,
don't do so in haste.
Take time to go through the discernment process again.
Talk it through with anyone who is affected by it and listen
    to their feelings.

Or are your regrets more to do with the cost of implementing your choice?

Perhaps you feel it has all proved to be much harder work than you expected.
Or maybe, after all, you can't bring yourself to make the hard decisions needed to implement your choice?

What lies beneath your desire to change your mind?

Is it, deep down, about a lack of courage in yourself?
Or is it about the demands of compassion for others?
Or is it fear of failure?

Look back to how you felt when you made the decision.

Was your inner compass really registering true north?
In your innermost heart, did you feel that this was the right thing to do?

If so, don't go back on a decision you took
when you felt you were really being true to the best in yourself,
now that your inner compass is starting to waver.

The choices we make when we are being most true
  to ourselves
should not be reversed simply because we hit times of
  challenge and difficulty, doubt and bewilderment.

If you chose this course when your inner eyes were seeing
  clearly,
don't change course simply because the fog has descended.
It isn't good navigation when you are at sea in a boat.
It isn't wise when you are at sea in your life.

Stay true to a course that you chose when your inner
  compass was giving you a true reading.

On the other hand,
if you made a bad choice,
at a time when your inner eyes were clouded
and your vision wasn't clear,
then it may be necessary to make a change,
if your existing commitments allow it,
if no one will be harmed by it
and if you have the courage to do it.

Before you reverse a choice you once made,
look long and hard
at what is prompting you to change your mind.

Is the nudge coming from a good place – for example,
a desire to improve things,
a desire to be more honest,
a desire to put right any harm that may have been done?

Or is it coming from a bad place – such as
fear,
resentment or revenge,
a tendency to vacillate?

The same wisdom applies as for the choice you first made:

What does the *best* in you choose to do?

A trusted friend can be a helpful mentor in trying to discern
just what the best in you *really* chooses.
Share your feelings – the good and the bad –
and as you talk things through,
you may hear your own true voice,
and your friend may be able to reflect the echo of that
    true voice back to you,
and help you to listen to its wisdom.

Moving on

Our choices in life become companions we have to live with.

It is liberating to realize that what is in the past
  cannot be changed.

You may go back to the same river again and again,
but you will never see the same water.

You may revisit old choices over and over,
but you can never relive that bit of your history.

Time moves on,
and we move with it.

The only thing we can change is the future.

So don't let your life be taken over
by the *what-if*s,
the *if-only*s
and the *might-have-been*s.

You need all your energy
to choose the way ahead.

The freedom to move on
means letting go of everything that holds us captive to the
    past.

It also means accepting the consequences of whatever
    decisions we have made.

Decisions can go wrong…

We can waste a lot of energy,
needlessly berating ourselves,
or wrongly blaming others, or circumstances,
for choices that we made ourselves.

This route only leads to reproaches and recriminations,
weariness and war,
war within ourselves or against the world.
It never leads to life.

Real freedom lies in the realization
that what is past cannot be changed.
Such freedom gives us the space to focus on what lies ahead,

changing what we can change,
accepting what we cannot,
and seeking always the wisdom to know the difference,

and remembering that in everything we do,
at every fork in the road of our journey through life,
however large or small,
we have a choice.

The choice is always about 'which way *forward*',
and it always begins right where we are.

Ten commandments for living true

1. Let the core of your being – your true self – be the place where your life is grounded.

2. Don't be content to live only in the outer layers of yourself, or allow any false self-images to become the ground of your being.

3. Don't trivialize your true self, or allow anyone else to do so. Don't trivialize the true self of another person.

4. Make space and time to discover and explore the core of your being.

5. Listen to the wisdom of your personal roots, and of the wisdom figures in your life.

6. Never do violence to your true self, or to the integrity of any other being.

7. Don't compromise your integrity by undermining sacred relationships. Live true to your relationships with other people and with all creation.

8. Don't steal energy by draining other people, but drink from your own well and share that well's water with others.

9. Don't say or do anything to present a false picture of your own core self or that of any other being.

10. Don't envy the gifts that belong to the core of another being, but nourish your own giftedness.